DATE DUE			OCT 0 6
GAYLORD			PRINTED IN U.S.A.

In Touch With Nature
Insects

**BLACKBIRCH®
PRESS**

THOMSON

GALE

San Diego • Detroit

**JACKSON COUNTY LIBRARY SERVICES
MEDFORD, OREGON 97501**

• London • Munich

PHOTOGRAPHIC CREDITS
Art Explosion: 1, 3, 5t, 6, 14–15, 22–23, 28b; **Image Ideas Inc:** 17; **PHIL:** 29br; **Photodisc:** 30; **USDA/ARS:** 4, 10, 12, 13, 19, 21, 24, 25, 27, 28t, 29tl, 29tr, 29bl.

Step-by-step photography throughout: Martin Norris

Front cover: Martin Norris and Photodisc

Consultant: Mark Hostetler, Ph.D.,
  Assistant Professor, Extension Wildlife Specialist,
  Department of Wildlife Ecology & Conservation,
  IFAS, University of Florida

For The Brown Reference Group plc
Editorial and Design: John Farndon and Angela Koo
Picture Researcher: Helen Simm
Illustrations: Darren Awuah
Managing Editor: Bridget Giles
Art Director: Dave Goodman
Children's Publisher: Anne O'Daly
Production Director: Alastair Gourlay
Editorial Director: Lindsey Lowe

LIBRARY OF CONGRESS CATALOGING-IN-PUBLICATION DATA
Available from the Library of Congress.

ISBN: 1-4103-0120-6

Printed in and bound in Singapore
10 9 8 7 6 5 4 3 2 1

Contents

What are insects?

Did you know?
Fairy flies are wasps that are so small they could fit through the eye of a needle.

Insects are among the tiniest of all creatures. They are also by far the most numerous. Experts know of more than a million and a half different kinds, and think there may be many times more yet to be found. More than 300,000 types (or species) of beetles scurry along the ground. Tens of thousands of kinds of bees buzz around flowers and make honey. More than 3,000 types of mosquitoes feed on other animals' blood.

Most insects are less than 0.25 inches (6 mm) long. Some fairy flies, though, are less than 0.01 inches (0.25 mm). The biggest insects are acteon beetles from Central America. They are more than 5 inches (125 mm) long and 4 inches (100 mm) wide.

"Medfly"
Like this tiny Mediterranean fruit fly, many insects have wings and are expert fliers.

CLOSE-UP *Grasshoppers*

Grasshoppers are insects that have big back legs for jumping. There are about 20,000 different species. Many can leap about 20 times the length of their body. If you could do that, you would be jumping 100 feet (30 m) or so! Grasshoppers are either short-horned, which means they have short feelers (antennae) on their head, or long-horned, which means they have long feelers. Short-horned grasshoppers feed on plants. Some, like lubber grasshoppers, feed on plants such as alfalfa, corn, and cotton. They are pests to farmers. Long-horned grasshoppers eat plants, too, but they may also feed on the remains of dead animals. A few pounce on and eat other insects.

Eastern lubber grasshoppers have big back legs. They move around mostly by crawling.

Insects come in many shapes and colors. But they all have six legs and a body divided into three parts. They are called insects just because their body has these sections. They have a head at the front, a middle section called the thorax, and a rear section called the abdomen.

Hard cases

Insects do not have bones. Instead, every insect's body is encased in a tough shell. This shell is called an exoskeleton. The exoskeleton is made from a substance called chitin (kite-in).

Unlike bones, the exoskeleton does not grow. Instead, it is discarded every now and then and replaced with a larger one. This process is called molting.

When an insect molts, it crawls out of its old shell to reveal a new one underneath. The new shell is soft, and the insect takes in air to blow up the new shell like a balloon. Once blown up, the new shell is bigger than the discarded one. It quickly hardens to form a tough shell again.

Did you know?
There are six billion insects for every square mile (2.6 sq km) of land on Earth.

Insect body parts

Did you know?
Nut weevils have jaws at the end of a snout, which can be as long as their body.

The head of an insect is like that of no other animal. It is made up of six different parts. On some insects, these look like steel plates on a helmet. On others, the pieces are so close together that they cannot be seen separately. What you can see are an insect's mouthparts, its eyes, and its feelers.

The shape of an insect's mouthparts depends on how it feeds. Insects such as beetles, ants, cockroaches, and grasshoppers mostly chew their food. Chewing insects have a pair of strong jaws called mandibles. Behind the mandibles are a pair of small limbs called maxillae, which also act as jaws. Often the mandibles have sawlike edges for slicing things. Insects such as aphids and butterflies suck plant juices. Others suck animal blood. Sucking insects suck through a long tube like a drinking straw. It is called a proboscis and is made up of a long, thin pair of joined mandibles.

CLOSE-UP *Insect structure*

Insects vary enormously in shape and structure. Some are very long and thin, like walking-stick insects. Others are flimsy flies. Bees have rounded bodies covered with thick hairs. Beetles are built like armored vehicles, with tough flaps, or wing cases, called elytra. The elytra close over the wings to protect them when not flying. Every insect, whatever its shape, has the same basic features: six legs, three body sections (head, thorax, and abdomen), plus feelers. Most have wings, too.

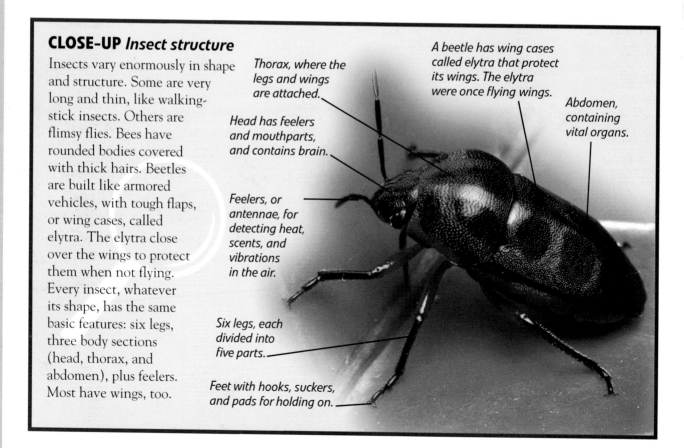

Thorax, where the legs and wings are attached.

A beetle has wing cases called elytra that protect its wings. The elytra were once flying wings.

Head has feelers and mouthparts, and contains brain.

Abdomen, containing vital organs.

Feelers, or antennae, for detecting heat, scents, and vibrations in the air.

Six legs, each divided into five parts.

Feet with hooks, suckers, and pads for holding on.

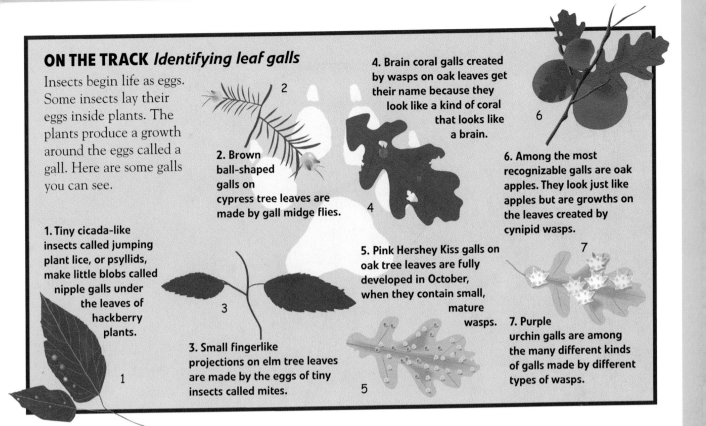

ON THE TRACK *Identifying leaf galls*

Insects begin life as eggs. Some insects lay their eggs inside plants. The plants produce a growth around the eggs called a gall. Here are some galls you can see.

2. Brown ball-shaped galls on cypress tree leaves are made by gall midge flies.

4. Brain coral galls created by wasps on oak leaves get their name because they look like a kind of coral that looks like a brain.

6. Among the most recognizable galls are oak apples. They look just like apples but are growths on the leaves created by cynipid wasps.

1. Tiny cicada-like insects called jumping plant lice, or psyllids, make little blobs called nipple galls under the leaves of hackberry plants.

5. Pink Hershey Kiss galls on oak tree leaves are fully developed in October, when they contain small, mature wasps.

7. Purple urchin galls are among the many different kinds of galls made by different types of wasps.

3. Small fingerlike projections on elm tree leaves are made by the eggs of tiny insects called mites.

Middle and rear

An insect's head is connected to its middle section, or thorax. The thorax is packed with strong muscles that move the six legs and, if the insect has them, the wings, too. Each pair of legs is attached to one segment of the thorax. Each leg has five main parts, with hinged joints between each part. Many insects have legs that are suited to their lifestyle. Water bugs and diving beetles have long, flat back legs that act like oars. Dung beetles have spadelike front legs for shoveling. Fleas and grasshoppers have big back legs for jumping.

Most adult insects have wings and can fly. Flies and mosquitoes have just two wings, but other insects have four (one pair forms the elytra in beetles). One pair is attached to the middle of the thorax. The other wing pair is attached to the rear segment.

The abdomen, at the insect's rear, holds the digestive system and sex organs. Insects look very different from other animals. But like others, they have a heart, guts, and a stomach inside their abdomen.

Many kinds of female insects, though, have something no other animal has: an organ called an ovipositor. This is a tube through which females inject their eggs into soil, wood, seeds, and even the bodies of animals. The ovipositor of many female wasps, bees, hornets, and ants has developed into a stinger. Males do not have stingers.

Did you know?

An insect's abdomen is made of 11 segments that telescope out so the abdomen can get much longer.

Collecting insects

The best way to learn about insects is simply to watch them. You can see them in your home, in your backyard, in the street, in fields—in fact, just about everywhere.

Many, like katydids, can be camouflaged so well that you cannot see them easily. So take time to look closely, and also to listen. Use the guide at the back of this book to help you get started in identifying insects.

To get a closer look at insects, however, you may want to collect them alive, and then set them free again. If you do collect insects, remember to treat them gently. Here are instructions for making a sweep net. This is a net for catching flying insects just above the ground, in grass, or around bushes and trees.

MAKING A SWEEP NET

You will need:

✔ Pliers
✔ Strong sticky tape
✔ Old pillowcase

✔ Broom handle or dowel
✔ Wire coat hanger

Did you know?
When a male cicada vibrates ribbed plates on its abdomen, the sound can be heard 400 yards (400 m) away.

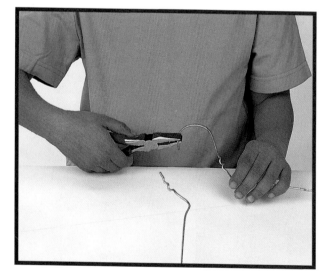

1 With an adult's help, use a pair of pliers to open up the wire coat hanger and bend it into a hoop about 10 inches (25 cm) across. Leave the ends straight for fitting the net handle later.

2 Feed the hoop through the hem of the pillowcase. You may need to cut a tiny slit in the hem to feed the wire in. If there is no hem, simply tape the pillowcase firmly around the hoop.

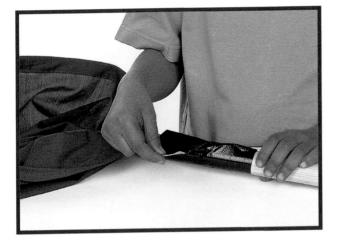

Catching insects

1. To catch insects, go out into a large grassy area and sweep the net slowly back and forth, just brushing the top of the grass. Tilt the open end of the net slightly down and forward.

3 Bend the two straight ends of the hoop together and lay them on top of the broom handle or dowel rod. Then wrap tape around the handle and the wire to attach the net to the handle.

2. Every half minute or so, swing the net quickly up into the air to force the insects to the bottom of the net. Then squeeze the net about a third of the way down to keep the insects from escaping. Carefully turn the net inside out to transfer the insects into a see-through container, such as a jar, a plastic food container, or even a plastic bag. Make sure your container has a small airhole so the insects can breathe.

CLOSE-UP *Observations*

Once the insects are in the container, look at them closely. First, try to identify the insects. If you cannot, do not worry. You can learn a lot about an insect without knowing what it is. Write down answers to these questions:
1. How many insects are there?
2. What does each look like? (What color is it and how many wings does it have, for instance?)
3. Does it crawl or fly?
4. Where did you find it? (Was it coming out of a hole or flying from a bush?)
5. What does it seem to eat? (Does it appear to feed on leaves or does it attack other insects?)
6. How does it behave?
Make regular sweeps in the same area and others at different times of day. Build up a picture of how insects live and what insects you can expect to see when.

Take care
Take care not to catch insects that sting, such as wasps. Avoid sweeping over flowers or lawns with clover.

CLOSE-UP *Bees and flowers*

Honeybees and flowers have a close bond. Neither would survive without the other. Bees make their honey from a flower's nectar, which they suck through their strawlike mouthparts. As the bee sucks, pollen from the flower gets stuck on the bee's hair. The bee combs the pollen off and presses it into "pollen baskets" on its hind legs. The pollen feeds the grubs (developing bees) back at the bee's nest. The grubs are not the only ones to benefit. Some pollen also gets brushed off the bee onto every other flower that it visits. The pollen is spread and other flowers are pollinated (fertilized).

Breathing and eating

Inside an insect's body, various systems work to keep the insect alive. Like all animals, insects must breathe all the time, and eat to live.

Breathing holes

Insects breathe, but they do not take air in through the mouth, as people do. Instead, they take in oxygen from the air through tiny holes along the sides of their bodies. The holes are called spiracles.

The spiracles are arranged in pairs, and insects have between 2 and 11 pairs. Each of the pairs is connected to a tube inside the insect's body called a trachea (plural *tracheae*). Each of the tracheae branches into smaller tubes. These tubes carry oxygen to every part of the insect's body and waste carbon dioxide back to the spiracles for breathing out. The spiracles normally stay shut, but they open to let oxygen in and carbon dioxide out. It is hard to drown an insect because, when it is under water, it closes the spiracles. This prevents water entering the tracheae. With air in its body, the insect tends to float.

Animal eaters

An insect needs energy to keep its muscles and body systems working. It gets energy from its food. When an insect swallows food, it goes into a tube. This tube runs right through the insect's body to its anus.

From the mouth, food slides down first into a wider area of the tube called the crop. There, it is softened by saliva. In insects that chew, it then moves on to part of the tube called the gizzard. An insect's gizzard has thick muscular walls that squeeze the food to break it up into small bits. Insects that suck have no need of a gizzard.

From the gizzard, the food goes on to a part of the tube called the stomach. There the food is finally digested. Nourishing parts of the food are absorbed into the blood. Unwanted parts go on down the gut and out through the anus.

CLOSE-UP *What insects eat*

Many insects are predators that kill and eat other animals. The prey is usually other insects, but mantids prey on quite large creatures such as lizards and frogs as well. Insects such as mosquitoes are parasites that feed off other living creatures. Many more insects eat plant parts such as leaves, fruit, wood, and seeds. Insects such as honeybees suck on the nectar of plants. Others, such as aphids, suck on plant sap. A few insects feed on rotting plants and dead animals.

Insects in flight

Insects were the first animals to fly—they took to the air about 300 million years ago. Like birds and airplanes, insects are lifted up by wings, but insect wings work in a unique way. Just as moving a hand quickly through water creates small eddies, so insect wings stir up small eddies in the air. The eddies lift them up. A few insects such as butterflies can glide by twisting their wings to ride the air. Most rely on beating their wings very fast. Even butterflies beat their wings 20 times a second. Midges beat them 1,000 times a second, much too fast to see. It is the sound of the wings beating that makes insects buzz. The faster wings beat, the higher the pitch of the buzz. The project below involves making a simple amplifier to hear the sound of insect wings beating at different speeds.

Flying aces
Many flying insects have four wings. Flies have only two wings, but they are the flying aces of the insect world. They can hover, change direction at will, and even fly upside down to land under a branch.

Did you know?
The fastest insects are dragonflies, which can fly at nearly 60 miles (97 km) an hour.

MAKING A WING-BEAT AMPLIFIER

You will need:

✔ Rubber band
✔ Scissors
✔ Empty plastic cup
✔ Waxed paper

1 Cut out a circle of waxed paper. Gently trap the insect you wish to study in the cup and cover the top with the paper circle.

2 Fold the paper down at the edges and secure the paper in place with a rubber band. Your amplifier is now finished.

Listening to the buzz

This simple amplifier allows you to hear the sound of the insect's wings beating surprisingly clearly. Different insects sound different because their wings beat at different speeds (see table, right). See if you can learn to recognize the sound of different insects. Release the insect once you have listened to it.

CLOSE-UP *Ladybug wings*

Many ladybugs are bright red with black spots. The number of spots varies with the species.

Ladybugs are tiny beetles covered in spots or stripes. They are popular with gardeners because they feed on aphids. Aphids are insects that damage plants by sucking their sap. A ladybug's spotted shell is really its tough forewings, or elytra, which protect the delicate rear wings beneath. The elytra give extra stability and lift in flight, but the rear wings give the real lift. When a ladybug wants to fly, it opens its elytra and unfolds the rear wings. Like all insects, it then warms up its flight muscles, either by beating the wings or basking in the sun. Once warmed up, the ladybug beats its wings faster and lifts off.

Insect	Wing beats per second
Butterfly	8–12
Dragonfly	25–40
Cockchafer beetle	50
Hawkmoth	50–90
Hoverfly	120
Bumblebee	130
Housefly	200
Honeybee	225
Mosquito	600
Midge	1,000

Insect senses

Every insect senses the world with the same five senses that humans do—sight, smell, touch, taste, and hearing. Yet these senses work completely differently in insects. An insect can hear with its feet, taste with its body, and smell with its feelers.

Hearing hairs

Insects have good hearing. Some can hear sounds much higher in pitch than humans can. Others hear sounds much lower. Yet insects do not have ears at all. A few, such as cicadas, have thin membranes in their bodies that detect sound like eardrums do. Most insects, though, do not even have these. Instead, they have sensitive detectors all over their bodies that pick up vibrations in the air, through the ground, or through plant leaves. The simplest of these are delicate hairs, like those on the feelers.

CLOSE-UP *Compound eyes*

Most insects have a pair of compound eyes made from many smaller eyes called eyelets packed tightly together. Some insect eyes have 30,000 eyelets. Each gives a slightly different view. All the views combine in the insect's brain to give a complete picture. Insects cannot move or focus their eyes, and only see things nearby clearly. Yet they can detect even a slight trace of movement, and see many colors. Most can see ultraviolet light, for instance, which humans cannot. Many adult insects also have simple eyes called ocelli on top of their heads. These help in flight and detecting light and dark.

ON THE TRACK *Identifying insect eggs*

Insect eggs are always tiny, but if you look closely you can often see them on leaves or on the ground.

1

2

2. Up to 50 cockroach eggs may be inside this case, dropped by a female.

3. Horseflies lay their eggs in soil or on rotten wood or dead plant stalks.

3

1. Eucalyptus tip bugs live on eucalyptus leaves.

4. Green lacewings lay eggs on long thin stalks sticking up from leaves.

4

Tasty feet, smelly feelers, touchy hairs

Most insects have the same taste sensations as humans—salty, bitter, sweet, and sour. But their taste organs are not all in their mouths. Many can taste with their feet. Bees and wasps can taste with their feelers. Wasps and crickets can tell where to lay their eggs with taste organs in their ovipositors.

The feelers, or antennae, actually have very little to do with feeling. Instead, they are used to detect smells. Although they cannot detect as wide a range of smells as humans, insects are very much more sensitive to particular smells. An emperor moth can smell a female more than 6 miles (10 km) away.

Insects sense touch with hairs all over their bodies. The hairs are so sensitive they can feel the air move. A fly is hard to swat because it actually detects the air being pushed toward it by your hand.

Did you know?
Cabbage white butterflies have a sense organ that responds only to mustard, their favorite plant food.

Insect armory

Insects are so small and plentiful that they are hunted and eaten by many creatures, including other insects. This is why some insects have developed poisonous bites or stings to help fight off attackers. Some harmless insects scare off attacks just by looking like insects that are poisonous. Many insects hide from their predators with color patterns that match their backgrounds. Others even look like something completely different, such as a leaf or a flower.

The most striking look-alikes are stick insects. They look just like sticks and make fascinating pets to study. There are about 2,000 species of stick insects, most of which live in warm places like India and Australia. They include *Pharnacia serratipes*, the world's longest insect. It is nearly 22 inches (555 mm) long, and comes from Malaysia.

KEEPING STICK INSECTS

You will need:

- ✔ Stick insects, typically Indian, available from most pet shops
- ✔ Aquarium or fish tank (or another very large glass container)
- ✔ Potting compost
- ✔ Spoon
- ✔ Needle or kebab skewer
- ✔ Empty plastic spread/cream containers
- ✔ Regular supply of bramble/blackberry leaves on stalks*
- ✔ Plant water sprayer
- ✔ Sheet of thin cardboard
- ✔ Sticky tape

1 Cover the floor of the tank with 2 inches (5 cm) of potting compost. Cut three small cross-shaped holes in the lid of each plastic container.

2 Fill the containers with water and insert your bramble stalks into the holes. Make sure the stalks are at least twice as tall as your insects.

* or Romaine lettuce, evergreen oak leaves, azalea leaves, bayberry leaves, eucalyptus leaves, or rose leaves

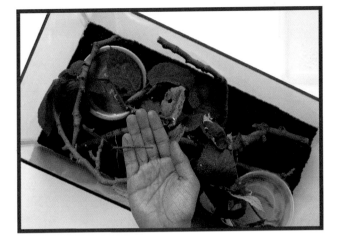

3 Now place the insects on the floor of the tank. Moisten the inside of the tank with a fine spray of water, taking care not to spray directly on the insects. Pierce holes in the cardboard and tape it over the top of the tank so the insects cannot escape.

Care of your insects
Keep the tank in a warm room (more than 60 °F or 16 °C). Moisten the tank with water every day and change the cardboard every week or so. Replace the bramble stalks when most of the leaves are eaten.

Observation
Stick insects are active at night. They sleep during the day when they are camouflaged by their appearance. Observe them hanging upside down to molt, once every month or so. See how they sometimes shed legs then regrow them. Some may even regrow heads.

CLOSE-UP *Chemical defense*

Many insects use chemicals against enemies. Bombardier beetles and other insects eject sprays of scalding chemicals. Stinkbugs, lacewings, and some grasshoppers emit foul-smelling chemicals called quinones or phenols. Bees, wasps, and ants have a stinger in their tails. Bee stings can be treated with baking soda. Ant stings can be treated with vinegar and lemon juice.

A wasp's bright yellow stripes warn others of its sting.

Did you know?
The bombardier beetle shoots attackers with jets of acid from the tip of its abdomen.

Insect life cycles

When they are adults, mammals look much the same as when they were born but bigger. Many insects change so much through their lives you can scarcely recognize them as the same creature. All begin life as an egg, but as they grow, they change in one of three ways.

Some insects change very little as they grow older. When the young hatch from an egg, they look like tiny versions of the adults. Every time these insects molt, they get bigger but look the same. Insects that follow this simple pattern include silverfish, springtails, and other wingless insects. These insects are scavengers. They are common wherever there are dead leaves and plants.

Half changing
Insects such as grasshoppers and mayflies go through a different process. The young of these insects are called nymphs when they hatch from the egg. They look much like adults, except that they have no wings. After a few molts, the wings appear. These

---

CLOSE-UP *A fly's life*

Houseflies are among the most widespread insects. Yet their lives are very brief. Female houseflies live for 26 days; males live just 15 days. But they reproduce at an astonishing rate. A female can lay more than 100 eggs at once. Her offspring can be ready to lay their own eggs just four days later. If all the offspring of a single female fly survived, she would have 200 million trillion descendants in just four months!

2. *Once they hatch, tiny, wriggling white larvae begin to feed on the rotting matter around them. They grow rapidly in three steps, or instars. In the third instar, they become mature larvae, or maggots, and crawl away to find soft ground for the next life stage, the pupa.*

1. *A female fly lays her eggs on dung, rotting meat, or plant matter. She uses her ovipositor to press them in firmly. The site will provide food for the growing larvae.*

3. *To become a pupa, the maggot buries itself. It turns its skin into a case, or puparium, around itself. The adult fly emerges a few days later, soft and crumpled, but fully formed.*

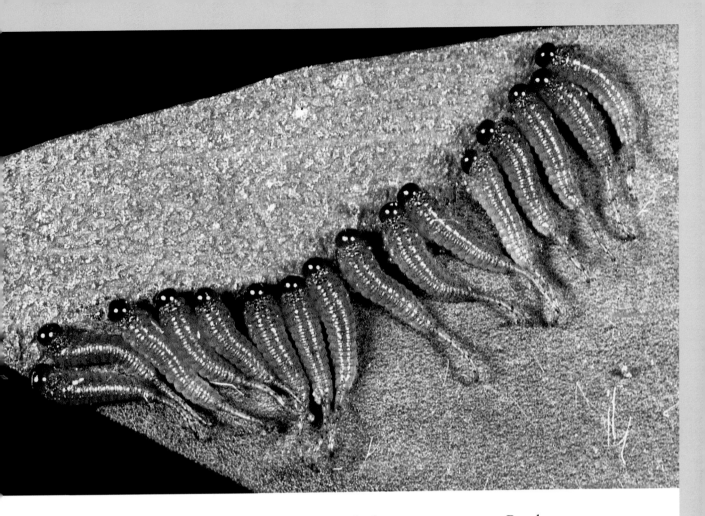

Baby insects

These might look like worms, but they are actually a family of insect young, called larvae.

are small at first, but get bigger with each molt. As adults, these insects feed on the same food they ate as nymphs. Insects like this are called exopterygotes, and the process is called incomplete metamorphosis.

Fully changing

Insects such as butterflies, beetles, and flies change dramatically through their lives. When they hatch from their eggs, they become larvae. Larvae look nothing at all like their parents and feed on different food. Most are soft, wriggling, and wormlike. Larvae of different insects have different names. Butterfly larvae are caterpillars and

fly larvae are maggots. Beetle, ant, wasp, and bee larvae are grubs. Mosquito larvae are wrigglers. When they are fully grown, larvae make a case, or pupa. Inside the pupa, the larvae change body shape completely and grow wings. Eventually, they emerge as adults. Insects like this are called endopterygotes, and the process is called complete metamorphosis. Many adult endopterygotes, like bees and butterflies, feed on flower nectar.

Did you know?

Botflies glue their eggs to mosquitoes so they hatch as the mosquito settles on a warm animal body.

Where insects live

I nsects live almost everywhere, from icy polar regions to lush tropical forests. Some insects can cope with temperatures as cold as -60 °F (-51 °C). Others survive heat warmer than 120 °F (49 °C). If conditions get too bad, many go dormant (shut down). They reawaken when things improve. As well as survival strategies like these, insects have a tough protective casing and can multiply rapidly. This combination enables them to live in more places than any other animal. Even the small area around your home has a wealth of different habitats for a huge range of insects. You might find ants in the soil, bees and butterflies around flowers, earwigs under rocks, flies around dung, fleas on animals, and many more. This project shows you how to make a pit trap to discover which insects live on the ground.

PREPARING A PIT TRAP

You will need:

✔ A shovel for digging in soft soil
✔ A large glass jar, or similar water-resistant container
✔ Pieces of fruit to act as bait
✔ Four small stones
✔ Piece of bark

Did you know?
Yucca moths can stay dormant for 20 years or so if conditions in the desert become too dry.

1 Choose a spot with soft soil where you think crawling insects may live, such as under bushes or in grass. Dig a hole large enough for the jar.

2 Put the jar in the hole so that the top is level with the ground. Pack dirt around it so that it fits snugly inside the hole.

3 Drop a little of the bait you have chosen into the jar. Lay four small stones on the ground around the top of the jar.

The pit trap
Drop a piece of bark on the stones so it covers the jar but leaves a gap so insects can crawl underneath and fall into the jar. Check the trap for insects at least once a day, since the insects may die if you leave them too long. If you find insects, take out the jar and empty the insects onto paper or into a small box to examine them closely as described on page 9. When you have finished, set them free again.

CLOSE-UP *Mud bees*

Not all bees live in hives. If you see a bee heading for a hole in clay walls and cliffs, it is probably a mustached mud bee. It is called a mud bee because the female builds a chimney of mud at the nest entrance, and mustached because the males grow a mustache in spring to attract the female. Unlike honeybees, mud bees only make a little honey. They mix it with pollen and body secretions to make "bee-bread" for their young.

Where insects live
● Ponds and marshes: mayflies, mosquitoes, water beetles and bugs, dragonflies, caddisflies, stoneflies

● In soil: ants, springtails, proturans

● Under rocks, boards: ants, termites, cockroaches, earwigs

● Flowers and leaves: bees, wasps, butterflies, moths, aphids, thrips, treehoppers, grasshoppers

● On animals: fleas, flies, lice, beetles

● In the home: clothes moths, house crickets, cockroaches, earwigs, ladybugs, silverfish

Did you know?
The fly *Polypedilum vanderplanki* can survive temperatures of 414 °F (200 °C), twice as hot as boiling water.

Insects through the year

More than any other animals, insects live according to the seasons. Mammals and birds live long enough to face all seasons. But many insects avoid hard times altogether by living only briefly. They go through their adult lives in just a few weeks. They can do this because they multiply rapidly to make the most of extra food available at certain times of year.

Every spring, in forest, field, and prairie, insects multiply with astonishing speed. Plant eaters make the most of the new season's plant growth, and predators hunt these herbivores. Bees and butterflies hum and flutter around the spring flowers. Crickets sing. Mosquitoes rise in giant swarms from marshes, and ladybugs hunt aphids that multiply on new green stems.

Some insects live longer and have to cope with winter. A few, such as monarch butterflies, avoid the cold by migrating to warmer places. Others go into diapause. That means they become dormant (shut down). Some insects time their lives so they pass the winter as eggs or pupae. These life stages do not need any food.

Honeybee queens and workers huddle through the winter in a ball in the heart of the hive. Flies, mosquitoes, and many other insects go dormant in caves and holes in trees. Insects' bodies contain a lot of water. To lessen the chances of freezing, some insects dry themselves out in fall. Others have a special antifreeze compound in their bodies that keeps them from freezing.

Every fall, insects that lay eggs find a safe, warm place to deposit them—in the soil, in wood, under rocks. The adults may not survive themselves. But their offspring will hatch the following spring.

A grasshopper's brief summer
Most grasshoppers live their entire adult lives in just a few short summer months. They emerge from their pupa only in late spring, then die shortly after mating in late summer.

Did you know?
The nymphs of dragonflies can survive in the water beneath the ice on a frozen pond.

ON THE TRACK *Insect larvae*

Some insects pass the winter as larvae. Most only emerge in the spring. Moth and butterfly larvae, called caterpillars, are big and brightly colored. Beetle larvae are yellow, fat, and are called grubs. Fly larvae, called maggots, are white and long.

1. Crane fly larvae have such tough bodies they are called leatherjackets. They live in soil and in wood, and eat roots and fungi.

2. Butterfly caterpillars can often be identified by their favorite plant. Buckeye caterpillars feed on plantains.

3. White or pale yellow blowfly larvae have tiny bands of spines around their bodies. They live in soil, leaf litter, or rotting wood. They eat the eggs, larvae, and pupae of other insects.

4. Horsefly larvae or maggots are tough and shiny. They live in wet soil or mud and eat worms and small shellfish.

5. Unlike maggots, beetle grubs have three pairs of front legs. The grubs of leaf beetles live on plant stems and leaves.

The social life of insects

Did you know?
Tropical tree ants can send up to 50 different chemical messages to each other.

Most insects live solitary lives. Usually, they get together only to mate. Some females guard their eggs and young for a while. A few beetles and bugs even feed their young. But most adult insects live entirely by themselves.

Social work

The exceptions to the lonely life are the social insects: termites, ants, bees, and some kinds of wasps. The insects live together and depend on each other for survival. They work together to find food, build the nest, take care of the young, and defend against attacks. Most live in big nests that they build to protect their young. More than 60,000 bees can live together in a hive. Millions of termites can live together in a single colony.

Dividing tasks

However many insects there are in each colony or hive, they are all the offspring of just one female. This female is called the queen. Her job is simply to lay eggs. Every other insect in the colony belongs to a group with a particular task. Most are workers, drones, or soldiers. None of the insects is told what to do; it simply knows instinctively.

Worker bees build the honeycomb and keep it filled with honey to help feed the colony.

CLOSE-UP *Bee hiving*

People have kept bees for their honey for thousands of years and have studied their behavior closely. Bees live together in nests in hollow trees or in hives made by beekeepers. Inside, the bees make a honeycomb of hexagonal (six-sided) cells divided by wax walls. The cells are storage pots for honey. The bees make honey to feed the colony when flower nectar is scarce. The cells are also bedrooms for the developing larvae. Beekeepers wear protective clothing when handling bees to avoid being stung. But not all bees sting. The queen has a powerful sting. So too do the workers that go out and gather nectar. But the drones that stay in the hive all the time have no sting.

Workers collect food, maintain the nest, and look after the young. Drones are males. It is their job to mate with the queen. Ant and termite soldiers are bigger individuals that defend the colony against attack.

The queen controls the colony. She oozes chemicals called pheromones. These tell the other insects they all belong together and keep the insects from mating with each other or with insects from other colonies.

Antics
There are thousands of different ant species. They all live together in big colonies and work together in remarkably complex ways.

Did you know?
Ants and termites make up a fifth of the total weight of all living things on Earth.

Insect homes

Insects are some of the most amazing builders in the animal kingdom. Some insects, like certain kinds of wasps, work alone to make simple shelters for themselves and their young. Social insects—termites, ants, bees, and many wasps—build elaborate nests. Termite nests are huge mounds that hold five million or more insects. Each nest has scores of chambers. Social insects build their nests from a range of materials, including leaves, plant fibers, mud, and wax. Termites cement together tiny pellets of mud with their saliva. Wasps make chambered nests from a papery substance. The wasps chew wood fibers into a kind of paste. Honeybees ooze wax to make the hexagonal cells inside their nests. This project shows how to make a formicarium, or ant farm, for studying ants' nests.

MAKING AN ANT FARM

You will need:

- ✔ Dry, sandy dirt
- ✔ Live ants, which you can buy from a pet or hobby store. Try to include a queen ant
- ✔ Large glass jar
- ✔ Small jar
- ✔ Thick, dark paper
- ✔ Cotton wool
- ✔ Bowl of water
- ✔ Cotton cloth
- ✔ Rubber band
- ✔ Sand
- ✔ Food for ants such as fruit and vegetables

Take care

If you prefer to collect your own ants, make sure you do not touch the nests of any stinging ants, such as fire ants. Ask an adult to help you identify the ants, and always wear gloves.

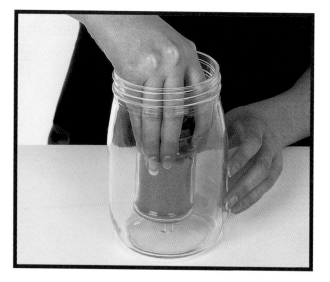

1 Fill the small jar with sand and put it inside the larger jar. This will force the ants to the outer surface of the jar, where you can see them.

2 Fill the jar with dry, sandy dirt. Put some food and a ball of moist cotton wool on top. Release the ants on the top of the jar.

3 Cut a piece of cotton cloth a little larger than the top of the jar. Secure it over the jar with a rubber band to keep the ants from escaping.

Care of your ants
Tape a piece of thick paper around the jar to block light. This fools the ants into thinking they are underground. Immediately, the ants will get to work on their new home and make tunnels. Leave them alone for a week to develop their network. Then remove the paper to see how they have progressed.

CLOSE-UP *Termite colonies*

Worker termites are white, blind, and wingless.

Like ants, termites live in large colonies, divided into groups, or castes. At the head of the colony are the king and the queen. The queen's abdomen swells hugely with eggs after she mates with the king. Soldiers are big termites who guard the nest. Smaller workers build the nest, forage for food, and tend to the young. Workers also look after the gardens of fungus the termites cultivate inside the nest for food. The nest is a huge mound of well-ventilated tunnels.

The ant farm
Be sure to place the ant farm in a bowl of water, just in case the ants find a way under the cloth lid and try to escape. Set the ants free after a few weeks.

Identifying insects

There are more than 1 million known species (kinds) of insects. But you can begin to identify any insect you see, by figuring out the group it belongs to.

See if you can fit it into one of these groups.

Crawling insects*:

 Termites: Pale, soft-bodied, and wingless; termites are seen in huge colonies.

 Ants, bees, wasps: Only ants crawl, but belong in the same group as bees and wasps.

 Beetles: Can be identified by their elytra, the hard, shiny forewings.

 Earwigs and cockroaches: Fast-running, brown insects that often have wings.

Two-winged insects:

 Flies: Small, very aerobatic insects with just two wings. Wings give low buzz.

 Mosquitoes: Tiny insects almost too small to see. Wings make high-pitched buzz.

Four-winged insects:

 True bugs: Bugs vary enormously, but many have flat, wide shape.

 Cicadas, hoppers, aphids: Vary in size, but their flat wings have no ridge as bugs' wings.

 Dragonflies, damselflies, mayflies: Fast-flying, slender-bodied predators.

 Grasshoppers, crickets: Have huge bent hindlegs for jumping, often colorful.

Mantids: Large long-necked hunting insects that often look as if they are praying.

*All these crawling insects fly at some stage in their lives. Adult wasps and bees fly all the time.

TERMITES

Social insects that live in colonies and build huge nest mounds. Mostly tropical.

ID clues:
- Short-bodied and short-legged. Long segmented body, rounded head.
- Usually wingless; only mating kings and queens have wings.
- Seen in large colonies.

> **Termites: Order ISOPTERA**
> There are 2,750 species of termites. They live in mud nests or underground mazes and feed mostly on rotting wood. They can attack house timbers.
> **Termites include: *Harvester, subterranean***

ANTS, BEES, & WASPS

Ants, bees, and wasps belong to the group Hymenoptera. All have narrow waists.

ID clues:
- Ants crawl along the ground, and have long, thin legs and feelers.
- Bees fly and have plump, furry bodies.
- Wasps have a pointed, stinging tail.

> **Ants, bees, and wasps: Order HYMENOPTERA**
> There are 198,000 species. Many are social insects and play a vital role as pollinators (bees), predators (wasps), and parasites (ants).
> **Hymenoptera include: *Black ants, bumblebees***

BEETLES

Robust insects with hardened forewings, called elytra, that meet down the middle.

ID clues:
- Look for the elytra.

Beetles: Order COLEOPTERA
There are more than 370,000 different species of Coleoptera, making it the largest of all animal orders. In fact a quarter of all the animals on Earth are beetles. They vary tremendously in size, from the tiny, barely visible feather-winged beetle to the gigantic hercules beetle of Central America, which can be more than 7 inches (18 cm) long. Most beetles are plant eaters, but they eat a huge range of plant matter, including leaves, seeds, hardwood, and nectar. Most live in leaf litter.
Beetles include: *Jewel beetles, stag beetles, ladybugs, rove beetles, fireflies, wood-boring beetles, click beetles*

FLIES

Small flying insects that live in almost every habitat, from caves to mountaintops.

ID clues:
- Two wings only, with rear wings reduced to two knobs called halteres.
- Large head and large compound eyes.
- Mouthparts for sucking.

Flies: Order DIPTERA
There are 122,000 species of Diptera, including mosquitoes and midges as well as flies. All flies eat liquid food, sucking through long mouthparts. Some feed on fresh fruit, some on plants, some on dung, and some on rotting meat. Because of their diet, they can often transmit diseases.
Flies include: *Houseflies, horseflies, robber flies, tsetse flies, vinegar flies, mydas flies, hover flies*

COCKROACHES

Cockroaches and earwigs are unrelated, but both scurry rapidly along the ground.

ID clues:
- Cockroaches have a tough, leathery covering and a flattened oval-shaped body the color of molasses.
- Earwigs have a distinctive pair of pincers called cerci at the rear.

Cockroaches: Order BLATTODEA
Earwigs: Order DEMAPTERA
There are 4,000 species of cockroaches and 1,900 species of earwigs. Cockroaches eat mainly rotting food, which is why they are sometimes found in kitchens. Earwigs live in soil and leaf litter and feed on plant matter and tiny insects.
Roaches include: *Madagascan hissing cockroach*

MOSQUITOES

Mosquitoes and midges are small, bloodsucking insects that are related to flies.

ID clues:
- Small, biting insects with high-pitched buzz.
- Midges often hover in smoky swarms under trees by ponds, bogs, and near the seashore.
- Mosquitoes have a needle-like proboscis for sucking the blood of living creatures.

Mosquitoes and midges: Order DIPTERA
Like flies, mosquitoes and midges belong to the order Diptera and eat by sucking liquids. Both mosquitoes and midges feed on living creatures. Midges have an irritating bite. Mosquitoes pierce the skin to suck blood, and often transmit disease.
Mosquitoes include: *Malaria mosquito*

TRUE BUGS

True bugs are a varied group of insects with generally broad bodies.

ID clues:
• Feelers bent in four or five sections, sucking mouthparts, wings with flat line across top.

True bugs: Order HEMIPTERA; Family HETEROPTERA
There are 36,000 species of true bugs, found all over the world. Many are crop pests.
True bugs include: *Stinkbugs, water boatmen*

CICADAS

Cicadas, hoppers, and aphids are oval-shaped insects that feed on plant sap.

ID clues:
• Aphids are small and green or black and have a tubelike tail.
• Male cicadas have a loud, chirruping song.

Cicadas, hoppers, and aphids: Order HOMOPTERA
The name Homoptera refers to their even-surfaced wings. Aphids can do great damage to plants.
Hoppers include: *Thorn bugs, froghoppers*

MANTIDS

Otherwise known as praying mantises, these are big predatory insects.

ID clues:
• Long necks and a way of holding their front legs together as if praying.

Mantids: Family MANTODEA
Mantids hunt by waiting motionless.

DRAGONFLIES

Dragonflies, damselflies, and mayflies are slender predators that live near water.

ID clues:
• Dragonflies, damselflies, and mayflies all have very long slender tail sections.
• Dragonflies fly fast and straight.
• Damselflies are delicate and flutter slowly.

Dragonflies and relatives: Order ODONATA
Dragonflies, damselflies, and mayflies are hunting insects that live near ponds and streams. Their young, called nymphs, live underwater for a long while before they emerge as adults. Adult mayflies live only one day, just enough time to mate and lay eggs. A mayfly is a nymph most of its life.
Dragonflies include: *Skimmer, darner dragonfly, darter, clubtail*

GRASSHOPPERS

Grasshoppers and crickets are large insects with powerful back legs.

ID clues:
• Huge back legs for jumping between plants.
• Often heard "singing" a chirruping song as they rub their back legs against their wings.
• Often bright green in color.

Grasshoppers and crickets: Order ORTHOPTERA
There are two main families of grasshoppers: short-horned (which includes locusts) and long-horned (which includes katydids). Crickets are relatives that make the same chirruping sound with their back legs. Katydids often look like leaves, which helps them hide among plants.
Orthoptera include: *Lubber grasshoppers, katydids, mole crickets, locusts*

Glossary

abdomen Rear part of an insect's body. Holds the digestive system, heart and breathing systems, and reproductive system.

antenna Long, thin, jointed sense organ on an insect's head, sometimes known as a feeler. Responds to smell, taste, and touch.

chitin Hard, flexible material of exoskeleton.

compound eye Eye that is made up of many tiny eyelets.

crustacean A small creature with a hard case such as a woodlouse, crab, or lobster.

drone A male bee that mates with a queen bee.

elytra The hard, rigid forewings of a beetle.

exoskeleton The hard protective outer casing of an insect's body that provides all its support.

formicarium A structure, or ant farm, built to observe ants in action.

gall Growth on a plant caused by an insect laying its eggs.

gizzard Section of a chewing insect's gut that breaks up food before it enters the stomach.

grub The legless larva of an ant, a bee, a wasp, or a beetle.

haltere Small, knoblike rear wings on a fly that act as stabilizers in flight.

larva The young stage in an insect's life before it undergoes complete metamorphosis to become an adult.

maggot The legless larva of some flies.

mandible The biting jaws of an insect.

maxillae Secondary pair of jaws developed from small limbs.

metamorphosis The transformation of a young insect into an adult in a series of stages.

molting The shedding of the outer layer of an insect's body as it grows.

nymph The young stage of an insect such as a dragonfly or mayfly that develops by incomplete metamorphosis.

ovipositor A tube on a female insect's abdomen used for laying eggs.

proboscis Tubelike mouthparts of insects that suck liquid foods.

pupa Last stage before becoming an adult in insects that undergo complete metamorphosis.

puparium The hard case in which a pupa changes to an adult.

spiracles Breathing holes in an insect's sides.

thorax The middle section of an insect's body where the wings and legs are attached.

trachea Branching tube that carries air inside an insect's body.

worker An ant, termite, wasp, or bee that finds food and looks after young but does not mate.

FURTHER READING:

Laurence Mound. Eyewitness Guide *Insects.* Pleasantville, MA: Alfred A. Knopf, 1990.

Christina Wilsdon. National Audubon *First Field Guide: Insects.* New York, NY: Scholastic, 1998.

Barbara Taylor, Jen Green, and John Farndon. *Bugs and Minibeasts.* Southwater, 2002.

John Farrand. National Audubon *Pocket Guide to Insects and Spiders.* Pleasantville, MA: Alfred A. Knopf, 1988.

Index